It's fun to draw

Sea Creatures

Mark Bergin

Author:
Mark Bergin was born in Hastings, England. He
has illustrated an award winning series and written
over twenty books. He has done many book
designs, layouts and storyboards in many styles
including cartoon for numerous books, posters and
adverts. He lives in Bexhill-on-sea with his wife
and three children.

Editorial Assistant:
Victoria England

HOW TO USE THIS BOOK:

Start by following the numbered splats on the left
hand page. These steps will ask you to add some
lines to your drawing. The new lines are always
drawn in red so you can see how the drawing
builds from step to step. Read the 'You can do it!'
splats to learn about drawing and shading
techniques you can use.

Published in Great Britain in MMXII by
Book House, an imprint of
The Salariya Book Company Ltd
25 Marlborough Place, Brighton BN1 1UB
www.salariya.com
www.book-house.co.uk

ISBN-13: 978-1-908177-56-8

A CIP catalogue record for this book is available
from the British Library.

Printed and bound in China.

PAPER FROM
SUSTAINABLE
FORESTS

Visit our website at **www.book-house.co.uk**
or go to **www.salariya.com** for **free** electronic versions of:
You Wouldn't Want to be an Egyptian Mummy!
You Wouldn't Want to be a Roman Gladiator!
You Wouldn't Want to be a Polar Explorer!
You Wouldn't Want to Sail on a 19th-Century Whaling Ship!

Visit our Bookhouse 100 channel to see Mark Bergin doing step
by step illustrations:

www.youtube.com/user/BookHouse100

Contents

Coral reef fish

 1 Start with a circle for the body.

you can do it!
Use oil pastels and smudge them with your finger. Use blue felt-tip for the lines.

 2 Add two large fin shapes and a tail.

3 Draw in the head and mouth. Add a small fin.

4 Draw in the eye and add a stripey pattern.

splat-a-fact
These fish are colourful and live near coral reefs.

crab

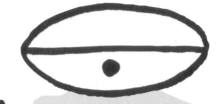

1 Start with an oval for the body. Add a line and a dot for the mouth.

2 Add two eyes on stalks.

splat-a-fact

Crabs walk sideways.

you can do it!

Draw the lines with a blue felt tip. Use coloured felt-tips to add colour.

3 Draw in the claws, one is much larger than the other.

4 Add eight legs.

6

Dolphin

1 Start with a banana shaped body.

2 Draw in the tail and add a fin.

splat-a-fact
Dolphins are mammals and breathe air, just like you do.

3 Add two more fins and the body marking.

you can do it!
Draw in the lines with a blue felt-tip. Add colour using coloured pencils.

4 Draw in an eye and finish off the mouth.

8

Manta ray

Splat-a-fact

Mantas are the largest and most spectacular of all the rays.

1 Start by drawing in the shape of the body.

2 Draw in two curved shapes at the front. Draw in the mouth.

3 Add lines for the gills and a pointed tail.

4 Draw in the eyes.

you can do it!

Cut up tissue paper and stick it down to make interesting textures.

10

Octopus

you can do it!
Use a felt-tip for the lines. Use oil pastels to colour with textured surfaces under your paper to get interesting effects.

1 Start by drawing a circle for the head.

2 Draw four curly tentacles.

splat-a-fact
Octopuses have 8 tentacles and live in rocky shores and tidepools.

3 Add two more tentacles.

4 Draw in two more tentacles. Add dots for eyes.

12

Flying fish

1 Start with a
banana-shaped body.

2 Add an eye, a line
for the gill and
a tail fin.

splat-a-fact

Flying fish make
long, flying leaps
out of the water.

you can do it!

Use coloured pastel
pencils and smudge
them with your finger.
Draw the lines with a
felt-tip.

3 Draw in two large fins.

4 Add four smaller fins.

Marlin

1 Start with the head shape. Add a dot for the eye.

2 Add a curved body and a tail fin.

you can do it!

Use watercolour paint to colour. Use a sponge to dab on more paint for added texture. Use a felt-tip for the lines.

3 Draw in a long, curved back fin.

4 Add smaller fins.

Puffer fish

you can do it!
Use coloured pencils and a felt-tip for the lines. Use scribbly lines to colour in.

1 Start with a spiky shape.

2 Add a mouth and two dots for eyes.

3 Draw in two stripey gills.

4 Add a tail fin and spikes.

splat-a-fact

Puffer fish are the second-most poisonous vertebrate in the world.

18

Sea horse

1 Start with the head. Add a dot for the eye.

2 Draw in the curved body with a curly tail.

you can do it!
Use wax crayons for texture and then paint over it with watercolour paint.

3 Add a spiky fin on the back.

4 Add spikes from its head to its tail.

Splat-a-fact
There are nearly 50 species of sea horse.

Seal

1 Start with a circle for the head.

2 Draw in two eyes, a nose and a mouth.

you can do it!
Use coloured inks and a felt-tip for the lines.

Splat-a-fact

Seals can hold their breath underwater for nearly two hours.

3 Add curved lines for the body.

4 Draw in two spiky flippers.

5 Add two spiky fins.

22

Whale

1 Start by cutting out the whale shape. Add a dot for the eye.

you can do it!
Stick down sweetie wrappers for the sea and torn white paper for the clouds.

MAKE SURE YOU GET AN ADULT TO HELP YOU WHEN USING SCISSORS!

2 Use a felt-tip to draw in the mouth and a blowhole.

3 Cut out the shape of the mouth from card. Stick it down.

splat-a-fact
To breathe, whales have a blowhole in the top of their heads.

24

shark

splat-a-fact
Adult sharks can swim up to speeds of 43 miles an hour.

1 Start with the body shape.

2 Add the tail fin.

you can do it!
Use wax crayons and paint over it for texture.

3 Draw in two large fins and three smaller fins.

4 Add an angry eye, lines for the gills and jagged teeth.

squid

1 Start with an oval for the head. Add the mantle.

2 Draw in the eyes.

3 Draw in four arms using curved lines.

4 Add another four arms. Draw two long tentacles with heart shapes at the end.

you can do it!

Colour with watercolour paint. Add ink to the sea and the body while the paint is still wet.

28

Turtle

1 Start with a round shape for the body.

2 Add the head and beak.

Splat-a-fact
The first known turtles existed 200 million years ago.

3 Draw in the arm flippers and back legs.

4 Draw in the eyes and beak shape. Add the pattern to the shell.

Index

www.salariya.com
where books come to life!

Download our free iPhone and iPad catalogue app. Search for Salariya or Book House

Children's non-fiction and graphic novels

Fiction for children and teenagers

Four free web books

Follow us on Facebook and Twitter

www.youtube.com/user/BookHouse100

The Book House blog – competitions, giveaways and current news